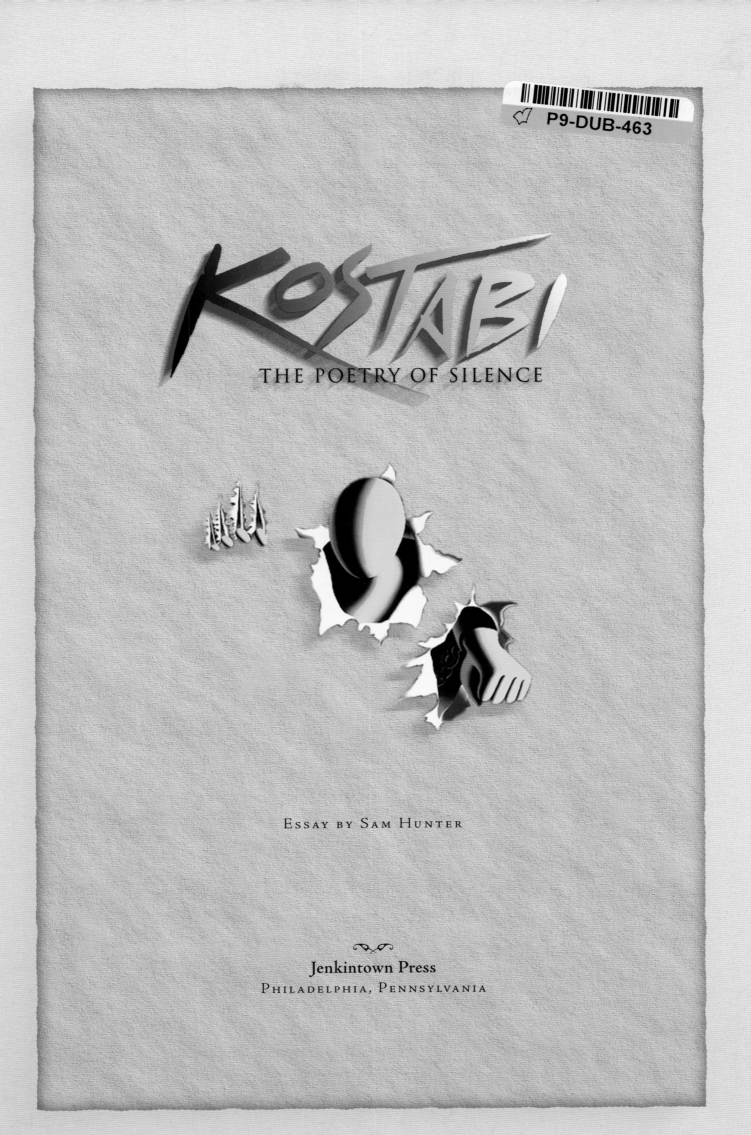

KOSTABI

THE POETRY OF SILENCE

Essay by Sam Hunter

Jenkintown Press
PHILADELPHIA, PENNSYLVANIA

© 1998 Martin Lawrence Limited Editions

Essay © 1998 by Sam Hunter
Interview © 1998 by Mark Kostabi

ESSAY
Samuel Hunter

INTERVIEW
Mark Kostabi

ART DIRECTOR
Gary Cohen

PRINCIPAL PHOTOGRAPHY
Hiromi Nakano

PORTRAIT PHOTOGRAPHY
Kimiko Yoshida

PRE-PRESS IMAGING
C&L Graphics, Van Nuys, California

LITHOGRAPHY
Color Graphics, Los Angeles, California

Library of Congress Catalogue Number: 98-65532
ISBN: 0-929460-12-X
First edition
Printed in the United States of America

All images © 1998 Mark Kostabi

Front cover:
Inner Circle (Coney Island), oil on canvas, 36 x 36 inches

IN A SENSE,
Mark Kostabi's works
speak for themselves. This artist
and his works are unique—in fact the
title *Poetry of Silence* almost seems an extension
 of the artist's persona. I hope you will enjoy the
journey through these pages and the insightful
comments by Professor Sam Hunter, who has been
able to place Kostabi, the artist and the man, within
the appropriate historical context. Kostabi has
made an indelible impression on the art world
and I have a feeling he will go much further.
It is exciting to be representing him at
this pivotal point in his career.
—DAVID ROGATH

Mark Kostabi's World

By Sam Hunter

 IKE THE EVERYMAN SUBJECTS SO CHARACTERISTIC of his artworks, Mark Kostabi is himself an intriguing, enigmatic presence, at once nowhere and everywhere in his art.

He willingly collaborates with the inventive, witty Italian Dadaist Enrico Baj or an even more challenging "outsider," the self-taught primitive Howard Finster, that manic man of the cloth and a widely acknowledged master of plywood cutouts and tractor enamels. On the other hand, he promotes himself openly, even shamelessly within the contemporary avant-garde, with its more stringent standards and artistic expectations, and then mocks his own familiar imagery and hides a truly fertile, fiendishly *au courant* cluster of ideas within the anonymity of an elaborate studio-workshop establishment where a talented corps of anonymous artists-for-hire actually execute his visual ideas, and attend his every command.

Adapting some of the most revered monuments of modernism, Kostabi has also wittily transformed Marcel Duchamps' legendary, iconic *Nude Descending a Staircase* into his own unmistakable version of a voluptuous Kostabism, its pliable form reminiscent, to be sure, of Pillsbury's earnest little doughboy. He has reconstructed his Everyman in new mythological garb as a modern artist mutating an immediately recognizable seated figure by Modigliani into his own preferred humanoid blob. Recently he even began to appropriate and restate within his own established stylistic mannerisms the angst-ridden gestures of the New York School's Abstract Expressionists of the fifties, in a painterly style that adheres to a fresh and virginal Kostabi format. And, ever unfazed and undaunted either by visual clichés or contradictions, at the same time he dangles a precisely rendered Meret Oppenheim's fur-lined tea cup from an imaginary studio ceiling in his homage-laden masterwork, *The History of Inspiration*, one of his truly impressive large-scale, summarizing paintings dripping with a smorgasbord of formal and immediately recognizable iconographic motifs recycled from modern art history and pop culture.

Equally crowded with signifiers of high modernist art are numerous familiar icons from the ubiquitous "imaginary museum" of art reproductions, in Andre Malraux's famous

Sam Hunter is an Emeritus Professor of Art History at Princeton University and the former Curator of Modern Art at the University Art Museum. He has achieved wide notice for his pioneering books and exhibitions of modern and contemporary art, including the first Jackson Pollock and David Smith one-person shows at the Museum of Modern Art, New York, where he was curator in the late 1950s. His recent publications include Modern Art: Painting Sculpture Architecture, *Third Edition, with John Jacobus and monographs on Marino Marini, Isamu Noguchi, George Segal, Larry Rivers and Tom Wesselmann. He was recently honored with the degree of Academician by the Brera Academy of Fine Arts in Milan, Italy.*

Mark Kostabi, *The History of Inspiration*, 1991, oil on canvas, 72 x 240 inches

phrase, that inhabit the bookstore-cum-giftshop in Kostabi's second great monumental study of recent years, *Counter Intelligence*, painted in 1996. This brilliant and riveting work is packed with readily acces-

Mark Kostabi, *Counter Intelligence*, 1996, oil on canvas, 84 x 144 inches

sible references to both the art products of the age, and Kostabi's own evolving oeuvre: multiple Duchamp readymades, such as his venerated bicycle wheel, some in sketchy, incomplete form awaiting production-line materialization, T-shirts adorned with Warhols and Matisse reproductions, while underfoot the great, saintly ascetic of modernist art, Mondrian, supplies a rug imprinted with the colorful abstract semaphores of his celebrated *Broadway Boogie-Woogie*, from the collection of New York's Museum of Modern Art.

These familiar, if not banal, images from the world of reproductions are a two-edged sword, however, reassuring to the art-literate viewer but also disorienting. They reaffirm the recent history of art, and its popular assimilation, even as they entirely divest it of the historical "aura" of genius and individual-ity, in the telling phrase of the great German critic Walter Benjamin. Kostabi's insatiable appetite for the Major Art Styles of Our Time is equaled only by the illusionistic skills of his studio assistants, or better, his execu-tors, who cleverly manage to reduce these famous motifs to their superficial, cartoon-like essence. Despite the liberties Kostabi and the shifting staff of painters beholden to him take in appro-priating some of the most exalted icons of the 20th-century avant-garde, a rather uncomplicated, serene mood of cheerful good will reigns supreme in Kostabi's New York studio factory. From this busy artistic production-line operated by hired helpers, and motivated in part by promotional ingenuity, pushed almost to the point of charlatanism, Kostabi has refashioned the practices of art-making in his time. His unabashedly collaborative enterprise overturns traditional notions of art-making and the values of personal creativity as we have known them, at least until postmodernist practices of "appropriation" and deconstruction took charge of professional art world practices.

Kostabi has placed his deliberately subversive imprint on the New York art world by joyously pursuing, and celebrating without qualms, commerce and personal recognition with equal degrees of focused energy and a Zen-like detachment

Andy Warhol, *Mick Jagger*, 1975, screenprint, 43½ x 29 inches

Sam Francis, *Untitled*, acrylic on paper, 37 x 72 inches

from the normative process of creating "original" works of art. His truly impressive self-promotional skills, insouciant spirit of anarchy, and at times even of wild abandon, in his wholesale appropriations of the art of his time, have come into full play ever since he boldly entered the New York art world in the early eighties.

As examples of his wide and impressive range of expression, and irrever-ent down-home humor, the stylized figure in *Moses Poses*, with its alliterative, punning title, cheekily lampoons the famous Michelangelo sculpture in Rome, *Moses in Chains*, perhaps verging on impertinence or even bad taste, while the more freely imagined, even rather ecstatic *Pilgrimage*, references Boticelli's *Birth of Venus*, and with consider-ably less competitive antipathy than the *Moses*. Kostabi *mostly* pokes good-natured fun at both the Old Masters and numerous modernists, among them De Chirico, with his enchanted, mysteriously vacant piazzas, and even the revered Picasso, in *Swimming to Guernica*. Here a truly curious, unexpected image reduces Picasso's great cubist mural—a prophetic, anguished visual document protesting modern warfare—to a bright and silly seaside sporting episode, representing a swimmer in an inner tube, reshaped into Picasso's famous dying horse. In fact, this visual invention should be taken not so much as a mocking critique of outdated anti-war sentiment at a critical moment in history during the Spanish Civil War, but rather as an effort to distance Kostabi's generation from a moribund, even suffocating modernist establishment which denied the values of "fun" and innocent pleasure, as well as the relevance of science-fiction fantasy. The latter reference can be deduced from the bather's headset. At worst, Kostabi is simply creating his own variation on a cartoon strip, more appro-priate to our age of pleasur-able narcissism. While the transformation may offend the serious art lover, it surely reflects a time in which pop culture and shallow entertain-ment values dominate public life, and art.

Kostabi's high-art image references have been so often reproduced that they have simply become part of a visual esperanto which he reshapes and rehabilitates, according to his own lights, with a remarkable adaptive facility. Even that master *farceur*, Salvador Dali, the most commercial of the Surrealists, becomes a Kostabi target, linked to American Pop Art. There are numerous other references to modern artists of stature in Kostabi's ouevre. A number, in fact, can be found, directly and indirectly, in the Picasso Blue Period drawing, "Spanish Peasants", Chagall's fantastic imagery, and, in an even closer fit, in comparing works by Magritte, Warhol and Keith Haring, selected at random from the history of modern and contemporary art. They make clear both Kostabi's roots in admired art historical precedent as well as his obvious ambivalence in appropriating some of its familiar iconic imagery. For the most part Kostabi uses the past as a ready-to-hand dictionary of ideas and motifs that his studio assistants, acting at his behest, can ransack, admiringly emulate or even profane, as the spirit moves the master craftsman and ideologue of his busy studio, Kostabi himself.

Keith Haring, *Pop Shop VI*, 1989, screenprint, 13½ x 16½ inches

At a earlier time in American art history, when the New York scene was still embarked stylistically, and emotionally, on an anguished neo-expressionism, Kostabi smoothed over the tactile qualities of his angular earlier works and recast their ambiguous subjects in a cool, almost clinical light, thus making a significant break with the dominant art style of The New York School. Turning to a deliberately plain, academic realism, removed from the style of fashion, he created sleek, stark images that are stamped with his own idiosyncrasies, as he communicated these elements and quirks to his designated producers of art diligently laboring in his anonymous "studio." In the following artworks which he seems to have the closest affinities are, at various moments in his development, Warhol's *Mick Jagger*, a Sam Francis abstraction, Chagall's *La Promenade*, and Keith Haring's equally cartoonish *Pop Shop VI*. Kostabi, who is a master assimilator, seems to have directly appropriated, and reinterpreted, figures from Magritte's remarkable painting, *La Reconnaisance Infinie*, with its mind-teasing, formally attired, bowler-hatted Belgian clerks adrift on a cloud. All of these quality works by famous twentieth-century masters, which have been taken by most aspiring avant-garde artists as iconic models of modernist "high" style, simply became grist for Kostabi's vernacular, imagistic mill. In his stripped down representations they are recast as curiously amorphous, sometimes mechanistic yet quintessentially accurate visual illusions with a striking, credible resonance and conviction.

In fashioning his own mercurial styles, and challenging the high modernism of his time, Kostabi set himself apart

Marc Chagall, *La Promenade*, tempera on board, 13¾ x 10½ inches

Rene Magritte, *Reconnaissance Infinie*, oil on canvas, 32 x 39½ inches

dramatically from the mainstream but positioned himself for success. Even his struggles became refreshing new material for winning attention: his earliest Everyman cartoon sketches, somewhat in the amorphous, agitated manner of James Thurber, were selling through his California dealer, Molly Barnes, when Kostabi set out to establish himself on the East Coast. He immediately began to network, "attending" every art event possible, reaching out to dealers and generally implementing the attitude he would later express in a pithy, if somewhat heartless, Kostabi aphorism: "There is no such thing as the unconquerable. Only the incompetent conquerer."

His fervent embrace of the methodology and mythology of success, in a world that was already commodifying the art object, was brash, but also disarmingly frank and certainly *au courant* in a delirious, inflationary art market that resembled the great Dutch tulip mania of the seventeenth century. If Kostabi is a paradox, he is also an amusing enigma. In the latest of a series of books he has published on his art and life, each as vigorously self-promotional and self-referential as the art they encompass, he elaborately documents his motivations and methods, sharing the secrets that have made him perhaps the most notorious *enfant terrible* of the art world since early Warhol.

From his ingenious practical applications, such as hiring young artists at minimum wage not only to create, or manufacture, his works but even to conceptualize and name them, he struck out on an independent path, apart from the commercial studios. He also exhorted himself and his workers with such irreverent slogans as, "A Dealer Should Not Have a Stable of Artists. An Artist Should Have a Stable of Dealers." With these strategies, and declarations, Kostabi has lifted the veil on the business of art, and gleefully parodied it with considerable financial success.

Yet, like everything else on the reference shelf and display panel in his studio-cum-factory, the words in the book he produced on himself, and by himself, called *Conversations with Kostabi*, both decode and deconstruct his art and life. Even as the artist introduces and explains himself, one senses that his circular discussion is a particularly ornate, playful way of elaborating what is already evident through the works themselves.

Above all, it is an irremedial sense of irony, and even a profound sense of disenchantment, rather surprisingly, that inform Kostabi's sly and potent genius. He becomes rather uncharacteristically impassioned as he comments on the dilemma of the contemporary artist in his book: "We are Kostabi figures," he states in a rather eloquent statement verging on a kind of doomsday surrealist vision. "We embrace a singular emptiness. Our power is like that of a lightning bolt that enters the earth, immense power dissipated in an instant. We steal only from ourselves.

"Our Buddha contemplates the unplugged appliance. We drink from empty goblets. The umbrellas are open but no rain falls. People watch TV, but the screen is blank. The world in my paintings is comfortable and familiar, but we have no place in it. It is our world, but we are not there." [1]

Paradoxical and elusive, such a reflection becomes powerfully poetic and, somehow, the glancing verbal equivalent of the images that are signed, or, as he says in the ever-present studio reader, *Conversations with Kostabi*, that are tagged with his name in the final, intimate gesture of his lapsed creative process.

He makes much of that holographic activity, as if to underline his imporatnce to the operation. Answering the question that he posed to himself, Kostabi explained that he does, in fact, sign every one of his paintings.

"And my hand is tired," he notes. "It's an absurd activity. Talk about irony. It's very ironic that the founder of a successful art studio is reduced to signing his name over and over, day in and day out. Paintings, prints, drawings, contracts, autographs, and checks. It's a primitive system of authentication that will eventually be obsolete, but it's the only system we have right now, so I play the game." [2]

Roy Lichtenstein, *Two Nudes*, color relief print, 48 x 41 inches

Not only does he play the game of commerce very well indeed, Kostabi also is the creator of what might be called the ultimate game of art, on a lofty, accomplished level that was set in motion earlier in the century by the great and always mystifying Marcel Duchamp and the Dadaists, and later ratched up a few notches by Andy Warhol and another of Kostabi's "heroes," the ever-popular, and brilliantly verbal David Hockney. In the nearly 20 years since he first made his mark on the New York art world, Kostabi and his industrious entourage have produced an immense body of work that is instantly recognizable as his own, and theirs, thanks to the clever and fortuitous "Everyman" symbol that evolved from his youthful fascination with cartooning, and from his need to objectify and systematize his meandering style.

Born and raised in Whittier, California, one of four children of Estonian immigrants Rita and Kaljo Kostabi, he grew up in what he described as "the Kostabis' comfortable American home, complete with a sectional couch (circa 1957)." [3] In his witty, scrupulously documented 1990 coffee table book, a weighty three-inch-thick volume that adopts and spoofs scholarly art writing, Kostabi traced the route from childhood to New York in late 1981 to "Kostabi World," the quite astounding art factory where an army of artists punched a timeclock and worked beneath such ambivalent messages as "Faster pieces are Masterpieces" as they faithfully manufacture Kostabi paintings by rote.

This remarkable career path, in retrospect, was clearly marked at every turn. Kostabi's ubiquitous figures are almost all featureless, as if they were raw material waiting to be stamped with individuality or, in an equally intriguing possibility, as if they had transcended specificity and become interchangeable parts in a grand design produced by an even grander machine, with Kostabi, by implication, in the all powerful role of *deus ex machina*.

Ciphers clad in the retro Spandex of Spider-Man lounge in the cool light of a club in *Snapshot*, blandly anonymous. In the two 1996 canvases that feature identical figures, *Oasis (Red Hot Lovers, Purple People)* and *Oasis (Tintoretto Tile Style)*, gestures are specific, but personalities are not. Around the central amorous couple, nose to nose with rubbery arms entwined, is a group of non-observers, oblivious to their physical links to one another: three diners have eyes only for their open laptop computers, while three others are absorbed in their cell-phone relationships, mindless clones adrift on the great communications superhighway of our time.

These images of contemporary anomie are quite as unsettling as any created by Edward Hopper or George Tooker, or even in another remarkable work, Roy Lichtenstein's witty invention from the comics, *Two Nudes*. Kostabi's paintings also resonate on other levels. Not only are all his figures, male and female, red, white or purple, equally faceless, they also have identically sleek, sinuously toned forms. In each work, the lovers' faces are forever separated, framed by the central column of arches that open onto a Renaissance courtyard. Around them are seamless masked forms that could easily be characters in some vapid play of manners, or in a cartoon whose caption has been lost or forgotten.

The figures appear charged with strong emotion, or can communicate deliberate frivolity. Aside from the stark and startling illusionism of their imagery, Kostabi's paintings capture the imagination, and linger on owing to the tension that vibrates between these alternate expressive possibilities. While the imagery is undeniably slick and mannered, it is also almost mockingly relevant in the process, and in its impact and stripped down visual statement, both overt and inherent. Much like Kostabi's impish characters in *Megaloma-*

niacal Regurgitations, the cartoon he drew 20 years earlier for his student newspaper at La Habra High School, called the Scotch Tape, they seem enmeshed in peculiarly unresolved situations. Today his more sophisticated figures in recent paintings enact a more resolved, single-image drama mutely, with no help from captions, unlike the bug-eyed, biomorphic creature in the prophetic but primitive high school comic strip.

Today Kostabi's figures command a wide range of expression and scenarios: they perform improbable gymnastic feats, sprout ungainly roots, illustrate, and, often deliberately defy their poetic titles, poke fun at corporate culture, spoof the working world, toy with masterpieces, offer variants on a good idea and, generally, raise questions about art in today's increasingly corporate and commercially-driven art world. In *By George*, two stylized profiles — one violently red, the other a high intensity blue — lean toward one another to merge into a small, discrete purple oval. Their bowed visages appear to penetrate the rim of a goblet in which a smooth burgundy wine gleams; over their blandly rounded heads, by contrast, is a jewel-like crown composed of the U.S. Capitol amid radiant floodlit beams. This vibrant cluster of national historical icons can be read, in the foreground, as a sensual encounter, or alternately a visual pun on George Washington astride a steed, in the background. The emblematic visual presentation helps distance the subject matter, much as Pop Art did with its veiled sarcasm and yet noncommittal, disengaged presentation of otherwise highly charged public imagery near and dear to the nostalgic, American heart.

Pablo Picasso, *Spanish Peasants*, watercolor on paper, 15 x 11 inches

The range of visual and social meanings expand in such works as *Acrobats (Aquarium)*, *Acrobats (Melba)*, *Acrobats (22nd Street)* and another related series of buff figures in motion, *Celestial Body*. In each, elastic genderless forms contort themselves into eye-catching configurations: one intricate pretzel-like figure perches on the other in *Acrobats*, while a single human form has been captured in the act of somersaulting in *Celestial Body*. Graceful, ethereal and ultimately improbable, their poses have more to do with an ideal of sublimation than athleticism, and they also seem to configure a Kostabian Golden Mean rather than corporeal truths.

At the same time, their position in a series of related works offers an amusing and satisfying dimension they would not otherwise enjoy. *Celestial Body* is poised on a white spotlight in *Moon Dance*, but then set against an exuberant Matisse in *Life Imitates Art*, the solidity of the figure and its existence in space established by the cast shadow. Other variants are equally decorative, and endlessly creative: one figure is poised with hands on a hoop, as a golden globe is balanced on an upraised toe; another is bathed in ruddy light

from a huge orb, a white ring whirling around an extended leg, frozen in the harsh theatrical light of a modern-day Caravaggio.

In variations on *Prance* a single figure stands silhouetted against a smoky nightclub scrim of blue notes; the strong sense of the dramatic is perplexing, however. At first glance the figures appear practically identical. Then subtleties emerge, thanks to the works' titles: one figure *(Ellington)* must be dancing to jazz; the other, *(Trip Hop)*, is surely jamming to something more "hip," a more energizing street rhythm. But other possibilities abound in these ambiguous works: the figure, apparently male, is without any identifying feature except a peaked hat that might belong to magician or clown, witch or dunce. His pose is open to interpretation, too: the light in each work is so mysterious and of such an exaggerated theatrical quality that he might be taken as a cartoon character simply tiptoeing by on some secret, furtive mission.

In the series based on the human hand, isolated in intricate poses in *Fidgity Digits*, *Mixed Signals* and *Fantasia For Four Hands* the imagery seems obvious and uncomplicated: hot-hued, strongly contoured exercises from a life class study.

Yet, just as strongly, other elements and a pervasive sense of mystery intrude. Despite their cheerful, graphic overtones, the work seems shadowed by some weightier intent. The arms that reach for one another in *Fidgity Digits*, and then make contact seem to belong to two different entities: one red, one yellow. Their ambiguity is profiled against a rainbow backdrop, frozen in gestures of longing and anxiety. As in *Fantasia For Four Hands*, a work composed of four panels in different spectral color combinations, the hands express a wide range of what might be taken as human emotions, besides the obvious tension of *Digits*, a desire to communicate and perhaps an urge to reach out, to make human contact.

What casts doubt on such fine parsing of the artist's intent, however, is the explicit denial of a credible humanity: however soft and detailed the digits, complete with wrinkles and veins, they are still disturbingly alien, or at least cloaked in Spandex, as it seems. Each hand ends in digits without nails, and, in a more sinister note, without finger prints. As if referring to their production method, they are rather beautifully realized, but they also tease our minds with their absence of any stamp of individuality. The hands, like the acrobats and lovers and other faceless yuppies and automatons that inhabit Kostabi's millenial America, are anonymous and unknowable.

The same intriguing mixed message pervades Kostabi's morality tales and interiors. Bone-white, with raised hands and outstretched fingers that resemble starfish, a man kneels in the gray, shadowy space of *Fight or Flight*. A white cat faces him, back arched and its curved form casting an exaggerated and expressionistic shadow. Both are clearly startled, although only two elements hint at the possible reasons: the glowing red outline that stains the shaded sides of both figures, and their nightmarish shadows. The man is a huddled mass, but the cat erect. Inexplicably, there is third shadow in this drama, cast by an imaginary figure from a different historical time warp. From its Napoleonic military headpiece to its raised rifle the shadow on the wall of a soldier identifies itself with Goya's grim execution scene, *The Third of May, 1808*, where a French infantryman points his lethal weapon at a cowering Spaniard, as if to confirm the human condition even as an apparently innocent civilian is about to be massacred.

Although the message seems very different in *Fight or Flight* and another 1997 painting, *Pink Room (Pacific Palisades)*, the style and tensions in the two works link them to the rest of Kostabi's oeuvre, and ethos. So reverential that he appears before a glass window-wall like a stiff statuette, a butler stands alone in the pink room holding a tray aloft. Soothing light and glamorous curves fill the space, which seems radiant with some raison d'etre that might justify its exquisite technique and air of satisfied self-importance. But all is gloss and surface in a work that makes no pretense about specific meanings: *Pink Room* is a spare but gaudy evocation of luxury, not visceral but merely lush and self-indulgent, perhaps an unintended ode to shallow material comfort.

The allusions that taunt, tempt and tease throughout Kostabi's voluminous oeuvre are nowhere more apparent, or entertaining, than in works that pay homage directly to modernist masters. In *Spring Cleaning*, the classic Kostabi figure, sleek in skin-tight white, bends and brushes butterflies under the earth-colored rug that also covers three standing figures. Other yellow butterflies drift along like greeting-card symbols of freedom, posed against a Magrittean sky of depthless blue dotted with soft, cotton-ball clouds.

Just as glib, and yet quite disorienting in its implications, is the 1997 painting/construction *Board with You*, a canvas that shows the two lovers of *Oasis, Apassionata* and *Brief Encounter* in a frustrating closeup. No longer mere Spandex-en-shrouded cyphers, they are now hard, richly grained sculptures in *Board with You*, only partly free from the wall and frozen forever in a clichéd sitcom embrace. The piece seems to comment slyly on a facile and exacerbated contemporary romanticism quite familiar to us from the steamy world of perfume advertisements. Reminiscent, too, of the early Magritte and his fantastic play with illusionistic surface patterns and textures, often emulating wood grain, it carries a distinct surrealistic jolt with its dissonances and contradictions. The painting/construction is also one of Kostabi's most skillful virtuoso exercises in technique. As a commentary on contemporary values it appears to be straining for sarcasm, but settles for a mere appreciative chuckle, if only because the male figure in the romantic equation wears a headset, as if he is already prepared to tune out the female he so ardently embraces.

Another impressive, larky Kostabism that skips through a full gamut of contradictory impulses, and then back again, is the painting *The Descendents*, a parody of Duchamp's once-galvanizing, revolutionary *Nude Descending a Staircase*. Kostabi has transformed this seminal 20th-century masterpiece into a stuttering, multiple-image improvisation: the "Nude's" Cubistic form is now sleekly clad in a pale lavender body stocking, it seems. Neither an out-and-out appropriation, and surely not an homage, the figure is a rather frivolous lighter-than-air confection that cannot seem to find a firm footing on Duchamps' slippery stair, or anywhere else in space. The figure is a fey, and flimsy caricature, and a rather pretty concoction at that, of the most scandalous work at the historic New York Armory Show in 1913, a veritable icon of modernism. Kostabi turns an art history monument on its head by transforming a bizarre hieroglyph from another age into a contemporary code, taken from the comics, which will offend the more serious advocates of modern art because it is, in fact, so innocuous and frivolous.

At the same time, even his mild sacrilege only underlines Duchamps' essential message: that art can be whatever the artist says it is, so long as the artist actually signs it and identifies it with his name. The spirit of Dadaism is alive and well, but obviously more kitsch than art. Kostabi's parody of an original parody is both irreverent and self-aggrandizing, and thus becomes yet another typical Kostabiism. Even his studio method of a modified form of deliberately depersonalized mass production takes essential modernism to its furthest limits, in a provocative reductio ad absurdum. Kostabi claims to have been stunned by the art world's incensed reaction to his advertisements in the eighties, which were perceived as insulting and demeaning. At that time he bombarded *The Village Voice* and other publications with rather shocking classified ad texts seeking workers for his studio, with "IDEAS for Mark Kostabi paintings" and for "realist painters…to execute lge, wet into wet oil canvases after drawings by Mark Kostabi."[4]

The requirements for the studio, obviously based on Warhol's factory but also more directly on actual factories, were specific: "Bring slides or origs to interview. Absolutely no expressionists. Bring resume if poss. $7/HR. M-F., 12-6. Please read ad carefully before calling,"[5] the ad stated, in terms that might be setting up some conceptual or performance piece, or simply a joke.

But Kostabi was *serious*, and entirely committed to his startling new form of artistic collaboration. Among the other gestures and actual objects that document his ongoing project are "Cue Cards from a Kostabi World employee training seminar;" these include such prompts as "Mister Kostabi and the Minimum Wage."[6] Kostabi reproduces paychecks to painter/workers in his factory, and captions a photograph of them in his unreservedly self-promotional coffee table volume as a group of "Limited-edition prints signed by Mark Kostabi."[7]

Other documents include examples of his self-created press kit, press clippings of his "attendance" at any and all art events of the eighties, as he created and orchestrated his public persona in New York. He also established himself through prints from his collection of portraits with famous people, including the snapshot of Kostabi embracing a standing cutout of former President Ronald Reagan as if it were the man rather than a cheap surrogate. At times, there seemed to be no limits to Kostabi's public self-abasement in associating himself with establishment values and entrepreneurial success, at least on the surface. Yet some of his more sophisticated associates and even critical supporters, including his much respected, long-time avant-garde dealer, Ronald Feldman, insisted that Kostabi was by no means merely a buffoon but, at worst, an *idiot-savant* whose parodic art and transparent PR strategies were, in fact, cleverly designed to subvert the philistine values of the establishment.

Kostabi also gave a prominent place in his warmly self-regarding book *The Early Years* to the ad for the Kostabi School of Painting that he claims to have placed in "high school yearbooks around the world,"° and to the image of himself at a machine, the KOSTAB-O-MATIC; he explained in a caption that mimics the solemnities of art scholarship: "Kostabi encouraged his staff to criticize his own method of production."[9] And he noted in the "fragment from *The Autobiography of Mark Kostabi*, draft. ca. 1980," that his ambitions arose early, came forcefully, and never abandoned him: "I want to have lots of fans who read everything that they can about me just like I did with my heroes.

"I hate to admit that I had heroes because I want to be THE BEST and if I have a hero then I'm not the best. So I don't have any heroes because I know that my drawings are the best and I know that they'll be in the news and magazines and after a while I'll have even more fans and there will be pictures of me with quotes," he wrote, allegedly and in a mocking, self-deprecating manner.[10]

In fact, throughout his career Kostabi insisted that he balanced dual emotions: the rage that drove him to work in a variety of mediums, from painting to writing to simply "attending," or appearing at every possible artistic venue of consequence, and being noticed; and a sly, irresistible wit. In his 1994 painting, *Office Deluge*, he shows a yellow figure shielding himself from an avalanche of modern technological equipment—fax machine, computer, clipboard, telephone. Painted as sleekly as the standardized products of his efficiently run art factory, it bears an abbreviated mock-Darwinian caption on its arched border: "SURVIVAL FOR EVERYONE AND BONUSES FOR THE FITTEST."

Even more pertinently, it features an agitated, rather touching message signed by Kostabi. "I'm searching within the giant cash register for that long lost achingly beautiful melody which haunted my childhood dreams," he (or one of his stable of painters, or an "idea" functionary) scrawled in acid green on a flat red backdrop. "I'm tormented by the inner demons of my fax machine eyes, the tortured soul of my digital Rolodex. For eons I stood in defiance against the ubiquitous agile timeclock."[11]

Kostabi is clear on the message's relevance. "It's a parody of phony spirituality as well as a parody of those who replace spirituality with business and technology," he has said, pointing out in an aside that he himself is devoted to art, and

not to business, despite his mask of public cynicism about art-making. "I spend 10 percent of my time doing business and 90 percent of my time creating art." "That's probably the same ratio as most successful artists. I just choose not to hide my 10 percent."[12]

And to cut corners and costs, Kostabi explained in the self-conceived, self-conducted interview, he appropriates material from many sources, and satisfies his creative urges. "I got most of the Tortured Soul verbiage from a music lecture I attended at the 92nd Street Y. I love it when people earnestly use that kind of over-the-top language. While at the lecture I copied down all the key buzzwords and later wove them in with business iconography instead of historical musical anecdotes."[13]

In Kostabi's words and argument, framed by his multiple personae as artist, businessman, public relations man, interviewer and respondent to his own probing questions, his personal legend developed and flourished over the past two decades because he also showed credible and abundant talent, boundless ambition and the necessary *chutzbah* to stand up to the abrasive, predatory New York art world. He has now securely established his visual vocabulary of smooth, glossy realism in concert with a deliberately banal academic execution, which also boldly embraced a wide range of social messages, so much so that he recently felt free to experiment in a radically divergent artistic direction. Today his turbulent, acrylic-splashed-and-soaked canvases surprisingly recall the works of the postwar Abstract Expressionists, as he has boldly reintroduced features that had vanished from his work around 1982: gesture and spontaneity.

He alternates his new series which is built around the flattened cipher of a flying, twisting, agitating acrobatic figure in space, and expressionistic paint handling with the more controlled styles and complex iconography that made his reputation here and abroad in the past. In either mode, he has retained the basic elements that first caught the startled attention of the international art world: the buoyant, athletic Everyman; the potential for mass-production in his commercially successful art factory, and, above all, the vivid sense of daring and fun that pervade his entire body of work. ∎

NOTES

1. Mark Kostabi, *Conversations with Kostabi*, (Boston: Charles E. Tuttle Co., 1996), p. 117.

2. Op. Cit., pp. 117-118.

3. Sir Basil Chattington, *Kalev Mark Kostabi: The Early Years* (New York: Vanity Press, 1990), p. 17.

4. Op. Cit., p. 84.

5. Op. Cit., p. 85.

6. Ibid.

7. Ibid.

8. Op. Cit., p. 105.

9. Ibid.

10. Op. Cit., p. 11.

11. *Conversations with Kostabi*, p. 134.

12. Op. Cit., pp. 135-37.

13. Ibid.

Mark Kostabi: A Self Interview

MARK KOSTABI: Where do you make your paintings?

MARK KOSTABI: Usually in New York City. But I create the ideas for them virtually anyplace. I divide most my time between New York and Rome and conceive many ideas for paintings while traveling throughout Italy.

MK: How do you get your ideas?

MK: Some of my ideas happen while looking at art (my own and that of others) in books and museums. Others occur while witnessing our society's obsession with technology—computers, cell phones and tomorrow morning's next gadget. After learning about conceptual art in art school during the late 1970s, I decided that my studio would be in my head. The quality and essence of my work is not the result of toiling away in a palatial studio with glorious skylights. Memory and confidence are my best art supplies.

MK: Where did you go to art school?

MK: Cal State Fullerton.

MK: You mean California State University, Fullerton

MK: Yes, the one near Disneyland.

MK: In fact, some people have compared you to Walt Disney. Were you inspired by him?

MK: A little. I was inspired by his relentless commitment to quality. But a Kostabi painting rarely resembles a Disney product. In the book, *Built to Last: Successful Habits of Visionary Companies*, by James C. Collins and Jerry I. Porras, the authors assert that Disney's greatest creation was not Mickey Mouse, Donald Duck, or any of his individual movies but the machine which consistently produced those products—the company itself with all its core values and ability to change with new demands. In that respect, one could say that I, with Kostabi World, the machine made up of numerous assistants and committees that consistently helps me produce my works of art, am like Disney.

MK: Who are some of your other influences?

MK: Everyone I encounter influences me in some way: cab drivers, composers, waiters, artists, art dealers, journalists, critics, presidents, etc. I am a product of my encounters.

MK: Who are some of your favorite artists?

MK: DeChirico, Caravaggio, Warhol, Antonella da Messina, Leonardo da Vinci, Lucio Fontana, Piero Manzoni, Enrico Baj, Mimmo Rotella, Picasso, Duchamp, Edward Hopper, Vermeer, De Kooning, Arman, Claire Falkenstein, Giacomo Balla, Enzo Cucchi, Louise Bourgeois, Carla Accardi, Arnaldo Pomodoro, Gio Pomodoro, César, Cindy Sherman, Rauschenberg, Yves Tanguy, Alberto Burri, Magritte, George Segal, Rodin, Bernini, Lichtenstein, Theodore Roszak, Anthony Caro and John Cage.

MK: Does music influence your art?

MK: Insofar as it affects my mood while I'm engaged in more spontaneous passages. However, it certainly influences my music. You know, I'm a composer and pianist, too.

MK: Yes, and your first CD of solo piano music came out this year, 1998. Who are some of your favorite composers?

MK: Stravinsky, Scriabin, Debussy, Satie, Fauré, Prokofiev, Pergolesi, Lepo Sumera, Astor Piazzolla, Khatchaturian, Lutoslowski and John Cage.

MARK KOSTABI IS ONE OF THE WORLD'S MOST CONTROVERSIAL ARTISTS, PROMOTING THE FACT THAT HE NEITHER PAINTS MOST OF THE WORKS THAT BEAR HIS NAME NOR CONCEIVES ALL OF THEM. STARTING FROM A UNIVERSE THAT MARK KOSTABI CREATED, HIS PAINTINGS ARE DESIGNED BY KOSTABI OR ONE OF HIS IDEA PEOPLE, EXECUTED BY ASSISTANTS, TITLED BY POETS, APPROVED BY COMMITTEES AND THEN SIGNED BY KOSTABI.

HIS WORK IS IN THE PERMANENT COLLECTIONS OF THE MUSEUM OF MODERN ART, THE METROPOLITAN MUSEUM OF ART, THE GUGGENHEIM MUSEUM, THE BROOKLYN MUSEUM AND THE GRONINGER MUSEUM IN HOLLAND. IN 1992 THE MITSUKOSHI MUSEUM IN TOYKO HELD A 100-PAINTING RETROSPECTIVE OF HIS WORK. RECENTLY, HE PAINTED A MURAL IN THE PALAZZO DEI PRIORI IN AREZZO, ITALY.

BORN IN LOS ANGELES IN 1960 TO ESTONIAN IMMIGRANTS, KOSTABI WAS RAISED IN WHITTIER, CALIFORNIA. HE STUDIED DRAWING AND PAINTING AT CALIFORNIA STATE UNIVERSITY, FULLERTON. IN 1982, HE MOVED TO NEW YORK AND SOON BECAME A LEADING FIGURE OF THE EAST VILLAGE ART MOVEMENT. HE DEVELOPED A PROVOCATIVE MEDIA PERSONA BY PUBLISHING SELF-INTERVIEWS WHICH COMMENTED ON THE COMMODIFICATION OF CONTEMPORARY ART.

(continued)

MK: *I've noticed that many of your recent paintings have references to music.*

MK: This is true because of my recent acceleration as a composer. Hitherto my paintings have been predominantly silent in feeling and volumetric with their razor-sharp linearity and tightly-controlled blending. Although the figures have been depicted playing musical instruments, there's been a silent stillness to my visual universe. However, recently I've developed a new style which I call template painting, which introduces a different kind of spontaneity and texture. A very painterly gestural style despite the use of templates, which imply mechanization and uniformity. They are created by dipping laser-cut steel templates of silhouette figures into multiple trays of paint and then stamping them onto atmospheric fields of paint on canvas, paper, or torn cardboard. One would not describe them as silent. The titles tend to be of a different nature as well. They usually have evocative one-word titles such as *Nimbus*, *Sojourn* and *Frontier*, whereas the volumetric paintings tend to call for two-word or phrase-like titles such as *Conversation Pieces*, *Upwardly Mobile* or *Reinventing the Self*.

MK: *So would you say there is a connection between the template paintings and your music?*

MK: Yes. Although I've composed music since 1977 and I've explored texture in painting from time to time, both the music and the template paintings blossomed at the same time, in 1997. Instrumental music tends to be more suggestive and abstract as are the template paintings. The volumetric paintings are more explicitly narrative. We could compare the volumetric paintings to music with lyrics.

MK: *Why did the template paintings and your music blossom at the same time?*

MK: Because living in Rome every other month away from the frenetic rhythm of New York art and commerce has given me the freedom to expand artistically.

MK: *Now that you're devoting a lot of energy towards the music and the template paintings will the volumetric paintings take back seat?*

MK: No, I drive a nonpolluting electric car with no gear shift so there's room for the three of us up front.

MK: *Are you saying that you don't pollute your body with alcohol, drugs or cigarettes and therefore have the time and healthy state of mind to pursue multiple directions successfully?*

MK: Yes, I could have said that myself.

MK: *You did. What was the inspiration for your recent series of square paintings called* **Inner Circle** *featuring your figures on a merry-go-round?*

MK: Giancarlo Politi and Helena Kontova, the editors of *Flash Art*, commissioned me to design a cover for their Italian edition. They gave me the idea to paint recognizable portraits of prominent artists riding on a carousel. Anselm Kiefer, Damien Hirst, Marina Abramovic, Vanessa Beecroft, Maurizio Cattelan and myself. The series you mention are faceless variations of the Flash Art cover painting. They speak of our society's embrace of conformity, while we go 'round and 'round again, brandishing cell phones and eating hot dogs. The omnipresent faceless figure in my work is both a reflection of society's fear of individuality and a universal visual language which empowers my work to bridge racial boundaries and allows the viewer to insert his or her own identify into the narrative. That's one reason why my work is popular in countries as diverse as Japan, Italy, Turkey and the United States. If I only painted nude white people, as do many famous figurative artists, my work would not be as globally communicative.

MK: *The exhibitions of your globally communicative art have enabled you to travel around the world. Where are some of your favorite places?*

MK: The garden at Villa d'Este in Tivoli, the Ryonji Garden in Kyoto, the sculpture garden of the Rodin Museum in Paris, Café Greco in Rome and of course my studio in New York City.

MK: *What is your ultimate purpose as an artist?*

MK: To improve the world by contributing as many interesting paintings as possible—and to inspire others to also realize their dreams.

Kostabi has designed album covers (Guns 'N' Roses' Use Your Illusion, The Ramones' Adios Amigos) and numerous products including a Swatch watch, computer accessories and limited-edition vases.

Kostabi has been profiled on 60 Minutes, Eye to Eye with Connie Chung, A Current Affair, Nightwatch (with Charlie Rose), The Oprah Winfrey Show, Lifestyles of the Rich and Famous, West 57th, CNN, MTV and numerous television programs throughout Europe and Japan. In print, he has been featured in The New York Times, People, Vogue, The Face, Playboy, Forbes, New York magazine, Domus, Artforum, Art in America, ARTnews, Flash Art, and Tema Celeste.

Kostabi lectures regularly worldwide and has published seven books, including Sadness Because the Video Rental Store Was Closed, Kostabi: The Early Years and Conversations with Kostabi. He produces a weekly cable tv show, Inside Kostabi, in Manhattan. Kostabi is also a classical composer whose music has been performed in New York, Japan, Italy and Estonia. ■

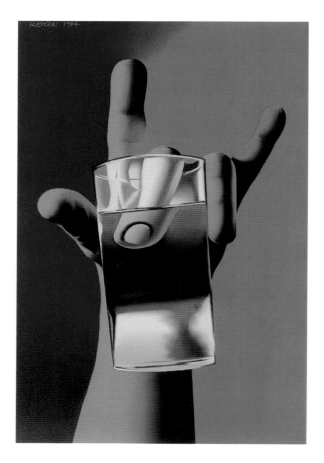

FIDGITY DIGITS
1994, oil on canvas, 34 x 22 inches

VISION THING
1994, oil on canvas, 24 x 16 inches

SIGN LANGUAGE
1994, oil on canvas, 28 x 40 inches

FANTASIA FOR FOUR HANDS
1994, oil on canvas, 28 x 40 inches

MIXED SIGNALS
1994, oil on canvas, 28 x 40 inches

INNER CIRCLE (Harmonics)
1997, oil on canvas, 36 x 36 inches

INNER CIRCLE (Dots All Folks)
1997, oil on canvas, 36 x 36 inches

INNER CIRCLE (Passing The Book)
1997, oil on canvas, 36 x 36 inches

BRIEF ENCOUNTER (Moonstruck)
1995, oil on canvas, 40 x 40 inches

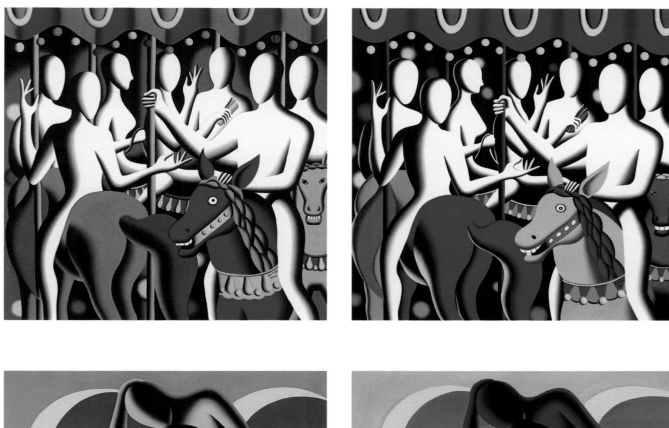

INNER CIRCLE (Lucky Seven)
1997, oil on canvas, 36 x 36 inches

INNER CIRCLE (Coney Island)
1997, oil on canvas, 36 x 36 inches

BRIEF ENCOUNTER (Capistrano)
1996, oil on canvas, 40 x 40 inches

THE SCARLET KISS
1995, oil on canvas, 40 x 40 inches

BRIEF ENCOUNTER (Urban Twilight)
1993, oil on canvas, 24 x 24 inches

TRIAD
1997, oil on canvas, 21 x 21 inches

MOVEMENT (Skybound)
1997, oil on canvas, 24 x 18 inches

MOVEMENT (In the Game)
1997, oil on canvas, 24 x 18 inches

MOVEMENT (Break Through)
1997, oil on canvas, 18 x 24 inches

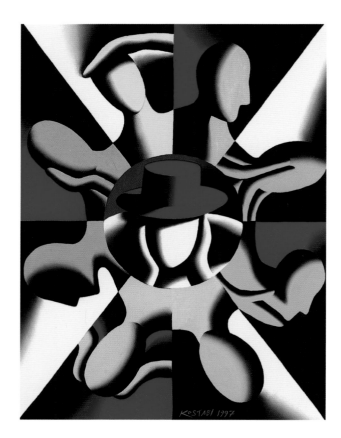

MOVEMENT (On Target)
1997, oil on canvas, 24 x 18 inches

MOVEMENT (Center Point)
1997, oil on canvas, 24 x 18 inches

MOVEMENT (Red Hat)
1997, oil on canvas, 24 x 18 inches

MOVEMENT (Circle of Confusion)
1997, oil on canvas, 24 x 18 inches

MOVEMENT (Atomic Hat)
1997, oil on canvas, 24 x 18 inches

MOVEMENT (Big Time)
1997, oil on canvas, 24 x 18 inches

MOVEMENT (Time Code)
1997, oil on canvas, 24 x 18 inches

MOVEMENT (Saturation)
1997, oil on canvas, 24 x 18 inches

ANIMISM *
1996, oil on canvas, 8 x 10 inches

SIGNATURE FACES * *
oil on canvas, 30 x 40 inches

ART OF THE DEAL (Terbium Defense) *
1996, oil on canvas with marker, 16 x 24 inches

*COLLABORATION WITH HOWARD FINSTER   **COLLABORATION WITH PAUL KOSTABI

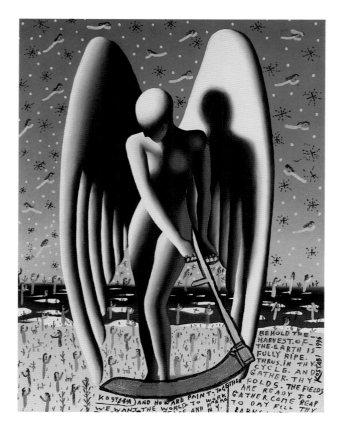

RANDOM HARVEST*
1996, oil on canvas, 24 x 18 inches

***ANGELIC RADIANCE**
1996, oil on canvas with marker, 24 x 18 inches

STRANGER OUT OF WATER*
1994, oil on canvas with marker, 10 x 8 inches

***REINVENTING THE SELF** (Red, Yellow & Blue)
1993, oil on canvas, 10 x 8 inches

*COLLABORATION WITH HOWARD FINSTER

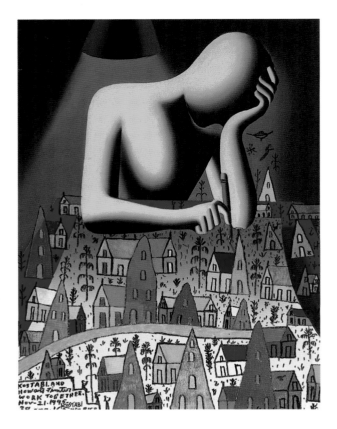

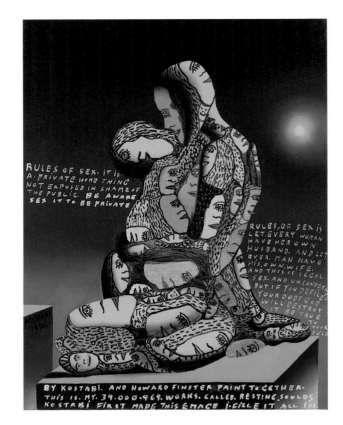

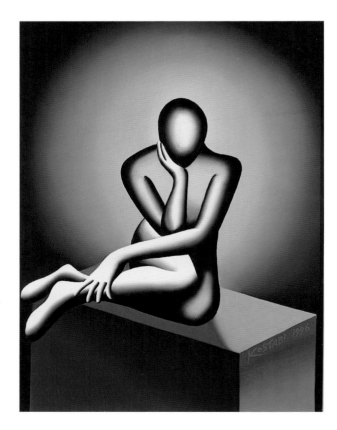

MONOPOLY *
1996, oil on canvas, 24 x 18 inches

***HOME THING**
1997, oil on canvas with marker, 24 x 18 inches

ALONE WITH AMERICA (Isolation) *
1996, oil on canvas with marker, 24 x 18 inches

SOUL AND THE SELF
1996, oil on canvas, 24 x 18 inches

*COLLABORATION WITH HOWARD FINSTER

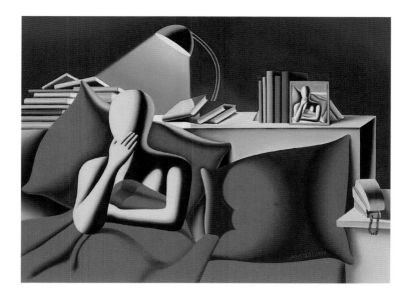

THE BACHELOR (Primary Focus)
1997, oil on canvas, 18 x 24 inches

THE BACHELOR (Open Book)
1997, oil on canvas, 18 x 24 inches

THE BACHELOR (Feline Persuasion)
1997, oil on canvas, 18 x 24 inches

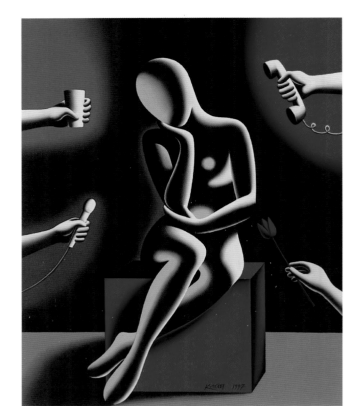

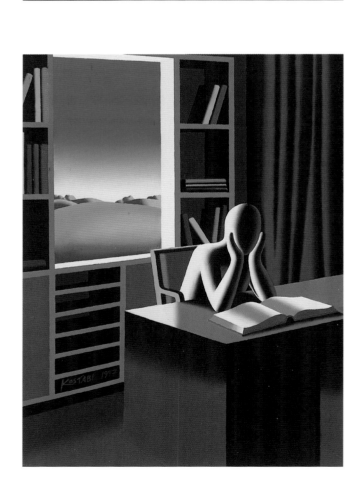

UPWARDLY MOBILE (Mental Block)
1997, oil on canvas, 30 x 24 inches

THE OPENING
1997, oil on canvas, 24 x 18 inches

USELESS KNOWLEDGE (Spring Break)
1997, oil on canvas, 24 x 18 inches

TREE OF KNOWLEDGE (Currency)
1996, oil on canvas, 30 x 24 inches

RING OF DESIRE (Classic Decision)
1997, oil on canvas, 24 x 18 inches

CELESTIAL BODY (Golden Globe)
1997, oil on canvas, 24 x 18 inches

AESTHETIC CODES (Fading Memory)
1997, oil on canvas, 18 x 24 inches

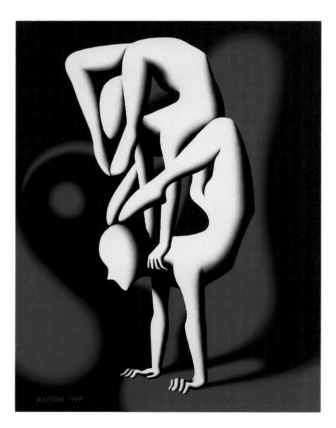

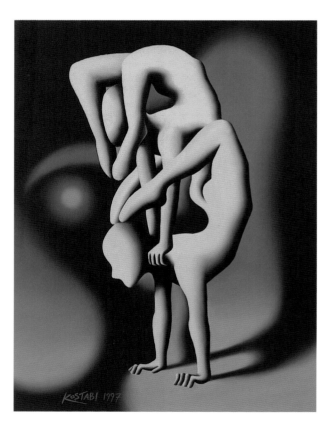

CELESTIAL BODY (Life Imitates Art)
1997, oil on canvas, 24 x 18 inches

CELESTIAL BODY (Moon Dance)
1997, oil on canvas, 24 x 18 inches

ACROBATS (22nd Street)
1997, oil on canvas, 24 x 18 inches

ACROBATS (Aquarium)
1997, oil on canvas, 24 x 18 inches

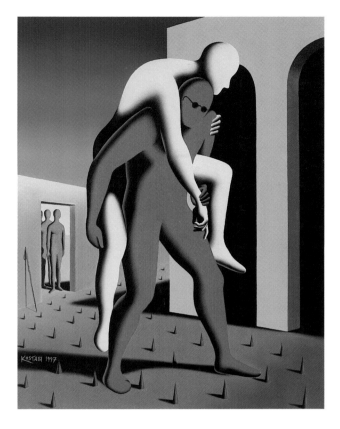

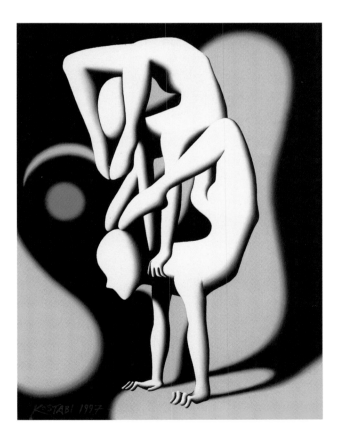

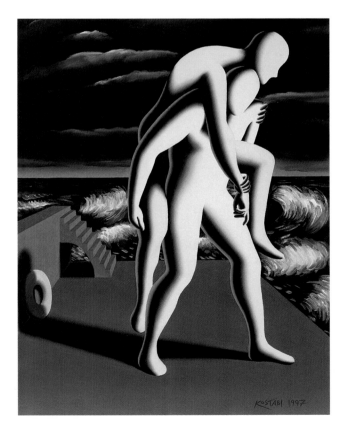

CELESTIAL BODY (Ring of Desire)
1997, oil on canvas, 24 x 18 inches

BACK AND FORTH (Next in Line)
1997, oil on canvas, 24 x 18 inches

ACROBATS (Melba)
1997, oil on canvas, 24 x 18 inches

BACK AND FORTH (Tempest)
1997, oil on canvas, 24 x 18 inches

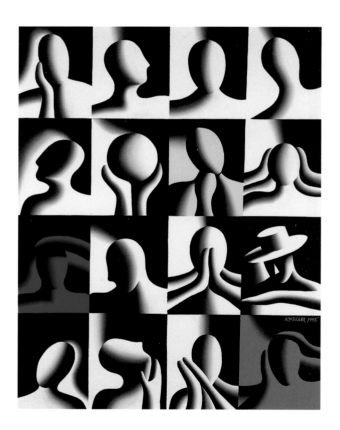

PRANCE (Trip Hop)
1997, oil on canvas, 24 x 18 inches

PRANCE (Ellington)
1997, oil on canvas, 24 x 18 inches

CONVERSTION PIECES
1995, oil on canvas, 60 x 46 inches

CONVERSATION PIECES (Grey Scale)
1997, oil on canvas, 40 x 30 inches

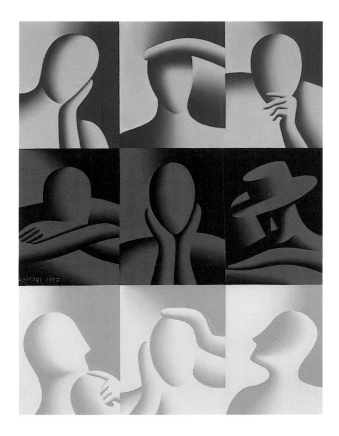

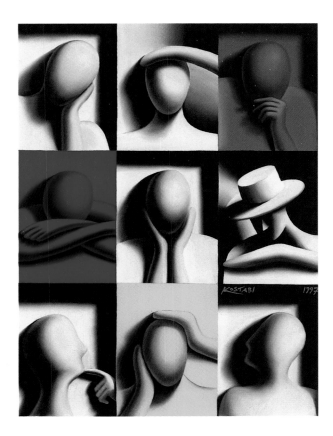

CONVERSATION PIECES (Blue Grey Days)
1997, oil on canvas, 24 x 18 inches

CONVERSATION PIECES (The Primarys)
1997, oil on canvas, 24 x 18 inches

CONVERSATION PIECES (Soft Focus)
1997, oil on canvas, 24 x 18 inches

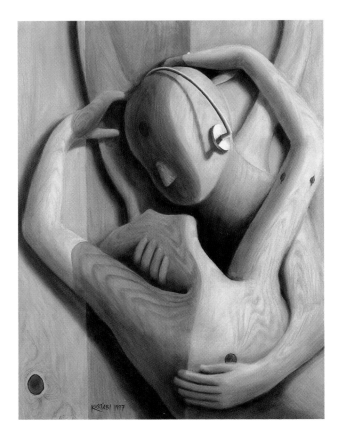

APPASIONATA (Rave Night)
1997, oil on canvas, 24 x 18 inches

BOARD WITH YOU
1997, oil on canvas, 40 x 30 inches

OASIS (Tintoretto Tile Style)
1996, oil on canvas, 30 x 24 inches

OASIS (Red Hot Lovers)
1996, oil on canvas, 30 x 24 inches

FEVER
1995, oil on canvas, 14 x 28 inches

DUETTO UN BACIO DITREVI
1997, oil on canvas, 20 x 20 inches

OASIS (Summer's Eve)
1996, oil on canvas, 30 x 24 inches

ANY OTHER DREAM (The Day)
1996, oil on canvas, 50 x 32 inches

MULTIPLE TRANSPARENCIES
1997, oil on canvas, 30 x 24 inches

IT PAYS TO ADVERTISE
1996, oil on canvas, 40 x 30 inches

TAX SHELTER
1996, oil on canvas, 30 x 24 inches

BY GEORGE
1996, oil on canvas, 24 x 18 inches

MONTE CATINI BIKINI
1990, oil on canvas, 40 x 40 inches

KICKING BACK
1995, oil on canvas, 36 x 36 inches

HEAD HUNTER
1996, oil on canvas, 30 x 24 inches

SWING CITY
1996, oil on canvas, 30 x 24 inches

RHETORICAL QUESTION
1996, oil on canvas, 48 x 40 inches

MOSES POSES
1997, oil on canvas, 24 x 18 inches

THE DECENDENTS
1997, oil on canvas, 30 x 24 inches

PILGRIMAGE
1997, oil on canvas, 48 x 48 inches

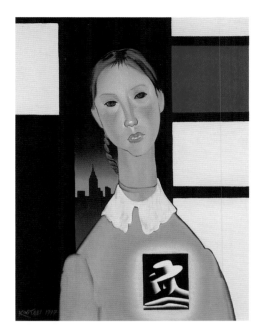

THE ENTITY MICHAEL
1997, oil on canvas, 24 x 18 inches

SWIMMING TO GUERNICA
1992, oil on canvas, 18 x 22 inches

CHAT ROOM
1997, oil on canvas, 30 x 40 inches

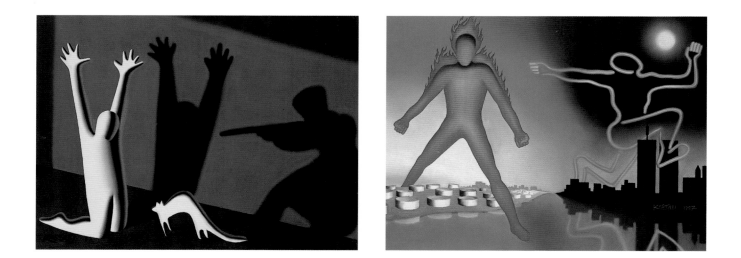

THE MODEL
1997, oil on canvas, 30 x 40 inches

LONDON CALLING
1997, oil on canvas, 30 x 40 inches

AS YOU WISH
1994, oil on canvas, 30 x 72 inches

FIGHT OR FLIGHT
1997, oil on canvas, 18 x 24 inches

BURNING AT BOTH ENDS
1997, oil on canvas, 18 x 24 inches

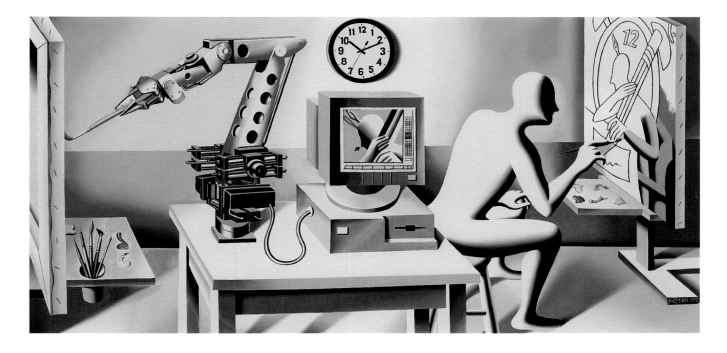

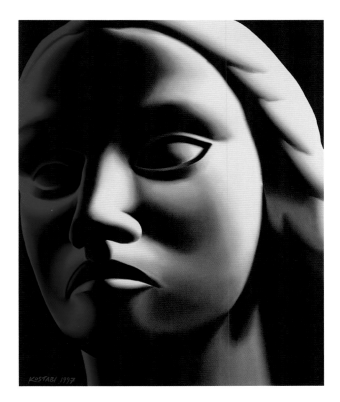

BEAT THE CLOCK
1997, oil on canvas, 30 x 60 inches

KHMER ROUGE (North)
1997, oil on canvas, 30 x 24 inches

RE-LOAD
1996, oil on canvas, 39 x 34 inches

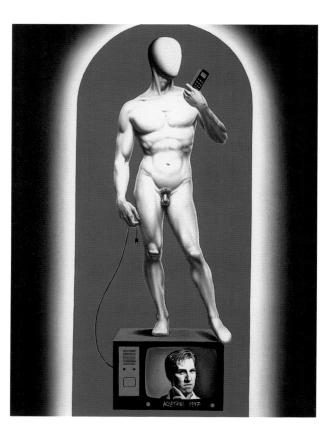

SATELLITE (Solar Flair)
1997, oil on canvas, 24 x 18 inches

SATELLITE (Shoot for the Stars)
1997, oil on canvas, 24 x 18 inches

BEYOND VIRTUAL REALITIES
1995, oil on canvas, 44 x 34 inches

PUBLIC ACCESS
1997, oil on canvas, 24 x 18 inches

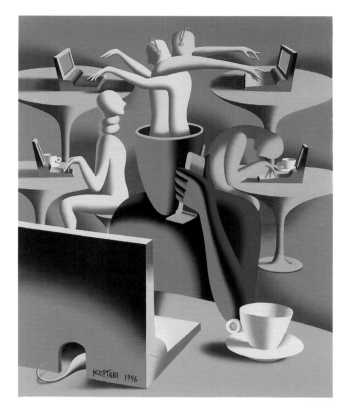

MESSAGE CENTER (Gold Rush)
1996, oil on canvas, 30 x 24 inches

MESSAGE CENTER (The Blue Light of Oblivion)
1996, oil on canvas, 30 x 24 inches

BIDDING AND BUYING
1996, oil on canvas, 30 x 24 inches

IM@.COM
1996, oil on canvas, 30 x 24 inches

WALL STREET STOMP
1996, oil on canvas, 30 x 24 inches

TICKER TAPE TRIUMPH
1996, oil on canvas, 30 x 24 inches

DIGITAL DERBY
1996, oil on canvas, 30 x 40 inches

FILTHY LUCRE
1992-96, oil on canvas, 56 x 48 inches

WIND-UP EXECUTIVE (Partly Cloudy)
1995, oil on canvas, 40 x 30 inches

WHEN YOU WISH UPON A BONE
1996, oil on canvas with spray paint, 30 x 24 inches

BUSINESS CLASS
1996, oil on canvas, 30 x 24 inches

SPELLING LESSON
1996, oil on canvas, 24 x 30 inches

BIGGER BUSINESS
1996, oil on canvas, 24 x 30 inches

LOBBING FOR DOLLARS
1996, oil on canvas, 24 x 30 inches

SERVICE ECONOMY
1996, oil on canvas, 24 x 30 inches

YOU ARE WHAT YOU SIGN
1996, oil on canvas, 24 x 30 inches

BOUND FOR GLORY
1996, oil on canvas, 24 x 30 inches

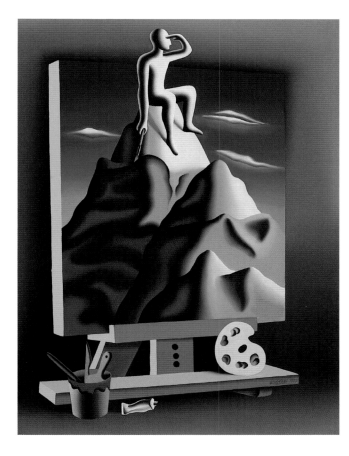

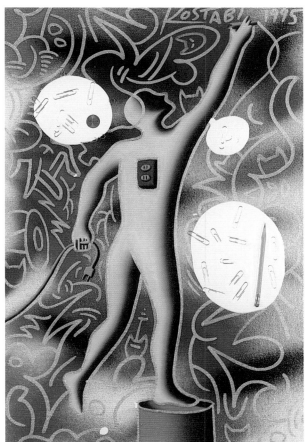

MAGIC MOUNTAIN
1997, oil on canvas, 40 x 30 inches

SPRING CLEANING
1997, oil on canvas, 40 x 30 inches

PAPER CLIP, PENCIL, PENNY
1995, oil on canvas, 24 x 18 inches

CONTAINER
1997, oil on canvas, 30 x 24 inches

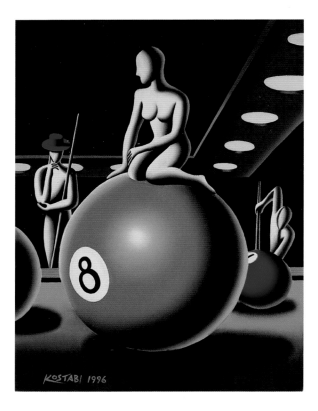

UPROOTED (Driver)
1997, oil on canvas, 24 x 30 inches

TO THE VICTOR
1996, oil on canvas, 24 x 18 inches

FAIRWAY TO HEAVEN (Par for the Course)
1996, oil on canvas, 30 x 24 inches

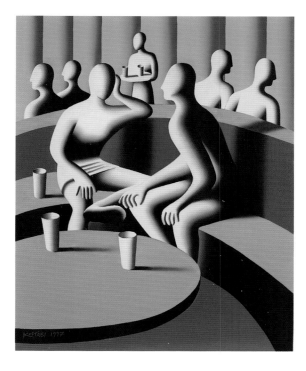

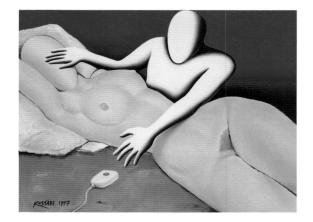

SNAPSHOT
1997, oil on canvas, 30 x 24 inches

CUMULUS LIGHTS
1990, oil on canvas, 30 x 40 inches

APPLICATIONS
1997, oil on canvas, 18 x 24 inches

ALIEN PRESENCE
1997, oil on canvas, 40 x 40 inches

EVERYMAN STAMP
1991, oil on canvas, 24 x 24 inches

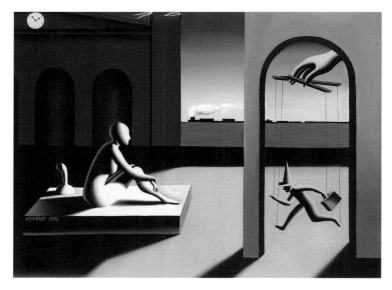

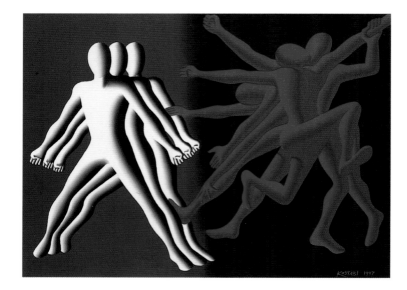

PUNCTURED DREAM
1997, oil on canvas, 24 x 30 inches

EXPECTATION
1996, oil on canvas, 36 x 48 inches

APOLLONIAN AND DYONYSIAN (Adagio)
1997, oil on canvas, 30 x 40 inches

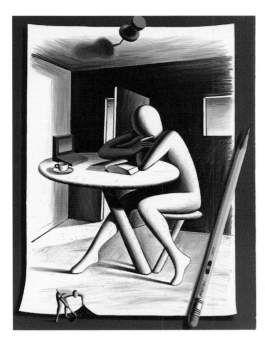

TRILOGY (Delete)
1997, oil on canvas, 24 x 18 inches

STARBOUND**
1997, oil on canvas, 30 x 32 inches

ORIGIN OF THE SPECIES
1997, oil on canvas, 18 x 30 inches

PINK ROOM (Pacific Palisades)
1997, oil on canvas, 26 x 30 inches

WHILE YOU WERE OUT
1990, oil on canvas, 36 x 48 inches

**COLLABORATION WITH PAUL KOSTABI

CONVERSATION PIECES
1997, screenprint, 20 x 16 inches, edition: 370

THE CELLIST
1998, screenprint, 20 x 15 inches, edition: 365

THE EARLY NERD GETS THE WORM
1993, screenprint, 34 x 34 inches, edition: 373

CLAUDE'S EXERCISE IN COLOR THEORY
1994, screenprint, 32 x 45¼ inches, edition: 376

CARBON CANYON
1997, acrylic on cardboard, 40 x 30 inches

NIMBUS
1997, acrylic on cardboard, 14 x 12 inches

VULCAN
1997, acrylic on cardboard, 14 x 14 inches

RELATIVITY
1997, acrylic on cardboard, 29 x 22 inches

FRONTIER
1997, acrylic on canvas, 22 x 30 inches

TRILOGY
1997, acrylic on cardboard, 28 x 40 inches

THRESHOLD
1997, acrylic on canvas, 24 x 16 inches

VERNACULAR
1997, acrylic on cardboard, 48 x 28 inches

KINEMATIC EVIDENCE
1997, acrylic on cardboard, 43 x 24 inches

TRANSUBSTANTIATION
1997, acrylic on cardboard, 37 x 22 inches

ANALOG
1997, acrylic on canvas, 18 x 19 inches

PROSPERITY
1997, acrylic on canvas, 40 x 20 inches

GLACIER
1997, acrylic on canvas, 28 x 22 inches

STRONG HOLD
1997, acrylic on cardboard, 27 x 23 inches

POLLENATION
1997, acrylic on canvas, 30 x 26 inches

MITOSIS
1997, acrylic on canvas, 30 x 24 inches

SEMAPHORE
1997, acrylic on cardboard, 45 x 20 inches

QUICKSILVER
1997, acrylic on canvas, 28 x 22 inches

TERRIGENOUS LIFEFORM
1997, acrylic on paper, 23 x 18 inches

PROMETHEAN
1997, acrylic on cardboard, 23 x 10 inches

INTERVENTION
1997, acrylic on canvas, 30 x 24 inches

RESOLUTION
1997, acrylic on canvas, 18 x 12 inches

SOJOURN
1997, acrylic on canvas, 44 x 26 inches

LA VIDA HOT SPRINGS
1997, acrylic on canvas, 36 x 32 inches

TRANSFERENCE
1997, acrylic on cardboard, 26 x 38 inches

CENTURION
1997, acrylic on canvas, 14 x 28 inches

TRIUMVIRATE
1997, acrylic on cardboard, 25 x 45 inches

Selected Solo Exhibitions

1981	California State University, Fullerton
	Newport Harbor Art Museum, Newport Beach, California
1982	Molly Barnes Gallery, Los Angeles
1983	Limbo Lounge, New York
	Simone Gallery, New York
1984	Molly Barnes Gallery, Los Angeles
	Limbo Lounge, New York
	Hal Bromm Gallery, New York
	Semaphore, New York
	Lucky Strike Gallery, New York
	Hal Bromm Gallery, New York
1985	Nada Gallery, New York
	Semaphore, New York
	Eastman-Wahmendorf Gallery, New York
	Semaphore & Semaphore East, New York
	Ray Hughes Gallery, Brisbane, Australia
	Australian Center for Contemporary Art, Melbourne, Australia
	Paul Cava Gallery, Philadelphia
	Art Awareness, Lexington, New York
1986	Seed Hall, Tokyo
	Folker Skulima Gallery, Berlin
	Ronald Feldman Fine Arts, New York
1987	Jan Turner Gallery, Los Angeles
	Freedman Gallery, Albright College Reading, Pennsylvania
	Wiesner Gallery, New York
	Peter Miller Gallery, Chicago
1988	Ronald Feldman Fine Arts, New York
	Philip Samuels Fine Arts, St. Louis, Missouri
	The Morgan Gallery, Boston
	Access Gallery, New York
	Hanson Galleries, San Francisco
	Tamara Bane Gallery, Los Angeles
1989	Fernando Alcolea Galeria d'Art, Barcelona
	Hanson Galleries, Beverly Hills and San Francisco
	Fly by Night Gallery, New York
	Hokin Gallery, Miami
	Alan Brown Gallery, Hartsdale, New York
1990	Govinda Gallery, Washington, D.C.
	First Gallery, Moscow
	Mijor Gallery, Kyoto, Japan
	Hanson Galleries, New Orleans and San Francisco
	Ronald Feldman Gallery, New York
	Ergane Gallery, New York
	Gross McCleaf Gallery, Philadelphia
	Gallery Sho, Tokyo
	Seibu, Tokyo
	Studio d'Arte Raffaelli, Trento, Italy
	California State University, Fullerton
1991	Art Collection House, Tokyo
	Galleria Dello Scudo, Verona, Italy
	Art Collection House, Osaka, Japan
	Frank Bustamente Gallery, New York
	Galerie Kaess-Weiss, Stuttgart, Germany
	Hama Gallery, Tokyo
	Access Gallery, New York
	Galerie 1900 – 2000: Marcel Fleiss, Paris
	Elisabettta Frigieri Arte Contemporanea, Carpi, Italy

	Paolo Majorana Gallery, Brescia, Italy
	Galleria in Arco, Turin, Italy
1992	Galleri Max, Stockholm, Sweden
	Martin Lawrence Modern, New York
	Sinimandria Gallery, Tartu, Estonia
	Mitsukoshi Museum, Tokyo
	Galleria Les Chances de l'Art, Bolzano, Italy
	Studio Spaggiari, Milan
	Galleria d'Arte Rizziero, Teramo, Italy
	Ginza Yamato Gallery, Tokyo
	Studio Cristofori, Bologna, Italy
	Vaal Galerii, Tallinn, Estonia
	Seibu, Tokyo
	Gio Marconi and Fondazione Mudima (collaborations with Enrico Baj), Milan
	PMMK Museum Voor Moderne Kunst (collaborations with Enrico Baj), Ostende, Belgium
	The Columbia Museum of Art (collaborations with Howard Finster), South Carolina
1993	Martin Lawrence Galleries, Washington, D.C.; Santa Clara, CA
	Hanson Galleries, New Orleans and La Jolla, California
	Galerie Kaess-Weiss, Stuttgart, Germany
	Santo Ficara Arte, Florence, Italy
	Centro d'Arte Moderna "Agatirio," Capo d'Orlando, Italy
	Azabu Museum (collaborations with Tadanori Yokoo), Tokyo
	Kobe-Hankyu (collaborations with Tadanori Yokoo), Kobe, Japan
	Multimedia Arte Contemporanea (collaborations with Enrico Baj), Brescia, Italy
	Cradle Salon/Aoyama Commons (collaborations with Linda Mason and Seiichi Tanaka), Tokyo
1994	Hanson Galleries, New Orleans
	Martin Lawrence Modern, New York
	Nicolae Galerie, Columbus, Ohio
	Studio Gastadelli, Milan
	Giovanni di Summa Galleria d'Arte, Rome
	Studio Spaggiari, Milan
	Sony Building, Osaka, Japan
1995	Dante Vecchiato Galleria d'Arte, Padova, Italy
	Guidi Galleria d'Arte, Genova, Italy
	Galleria Blu Art, Teramo, Italy
	Martin Lawrence Modern, New York
	Galerie Sho, Tokyo
1996	Centro Arte, Milan
	Elisabetta Frigieri Arte Contemporanea, Sassuolo, Italy
	Neuffer AmPark, Pirmasens, Germany
	Martin Lawrence Galleries, Chicago and Oakbrook, Illinois and King of Prussia, Pennsylvania
	Nicolae Galerie, Columbus, Ohio
1997	Oprandi Arte Contemporanea, Boltiere, Italy
	Scola dei Tiraoro e Battioro, Venice, Italy
	Martin Lawrence Galleries, Los Angeles, Newport Beach, San Francisco and New York
	Castello Doria, Porto Venere, Italy
	Galleria Nuova Gissi, Turin, Italy
	Galleria d'Arte Moderna "Il Castello," Milan
1998	L'Immagine Galleria d'Arte Contemporanea, Arezzo, Italy
	Ferrara Arte, Ferrara, Italy
	Blu Art Arte Moderna, Alba Adriatica, Italy
	Galleria Arte Rotaross, Novara, Italy